A
Son
is a
Gift

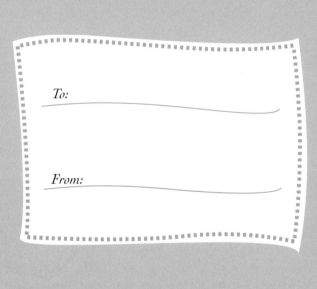

To:
_____

From:
_____

A Son is a Gift

Illustrated by Alexis Siroc

WARNER BOOKS

An AOL Time Warner Company

Warner Book, Inc., 1271 Avenue of the Americas, New York, NY 10020

Visit our Web site at www.twbookmark.com.

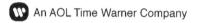 An AOL Time Warner Company

Printed in the United States of America

First Printing: April 2003

10 9 8 7 6 5 4 3 2 1

Library of Congress Cataloging-in-Publication Data

A son is a gift.

    p.cm.

  ISBN 0-446-53119-7

    1. Sons. 2. Fathers and sons. 3. Gift books. I. Warner Books (Firm)

  HQ775 .S66 2003

  306.874--dc21

                                   2002033109

Design by Alexis Siroc

The wildest colts make the best horses.

—THEMISTOCLES

A Son is a Gift

"*And all to leave what with his toil he won*

To that unfeather'd two-legged thing—a son."

—JOHN DRYDEN

*I*magine, if you can, a tiny boy kneeling in the center of a sandbox, wearing a faded pair of blue denim overalls.

Maybe he's a "wheelie" boy who races cars and trucks all day on ramps and roadways set into the dunes. Or maybe he's a sandbox warrior who uses homemade sound effects to blow up "bad guys" hidden in "enemy camps." Perhaps our boy is a dinosaur hunter fascinated by massive jawbones and giant wingspans that allow his armada of reptiles to win the battle of survival. Or maybe he's a budding archaeologist who treats bottle caps and bits of glass like precious booty pinched from the pyramids.

You gaze upon this boy, who builds and dismantles, makes war and peace, wipes out entire species, and plays every part in every game. You gaze on him as only you can, remembering the first time you held him in your arms and fell in love. Because, you see, he isn't any little boy. He is *your* little boy—your *son*. And the picture is perfect.

A son is a gift. Whether those words have ever filtered through your mind or rolled off your tongue in a quiet moment of deep reflection, the truth is undeniable. A son is a gift of extraordinary value. Serving as keeper of the family name and guardian of its promise, a son breathes new life into old plans and reminds the world of what tomorrow may bring. As the author of Genesis wrote so many centuries ago, "The smell of my son is the smell of a field which the Lord has blessed." Bearing the promise of a new harvest, a son carries forward the cycle of life and the splendor of regeneration.

What gives our sons such prowess and mystique, making them standard bearers of possibilities? Perhaps Renaissance man Francis Bacon put his finger on it in his

...in the sandbox, where they reign like tiny gods...

essay "Of Youth and Age," written in 1620. Illuminating the differences between fathers and sons, Bacon observed that "men of age object too much, consult too long, adventure too little, respond too soon and seldom drive business home to the full period but content themselves with the mediocrity of success." Sons, Bacon continues, are different. "In the conduct and management of their actions," he writes, "they embrace more than they can hold, stir more than they can quiet and go to the end without considerations of the means and degrees."

To put it plainly, our sons push the limits and stir the pot. Fueled by the spirit of adventure and the vibrant energy of youth, they reach for the stars, fearlessly going where none has gone before. Scoffing at cautions to play it safe, they blaze new trails and skate on thin ice. Challenging tradition and authority, our sons thrill to the "no fear" motto of the snowboarding culture that proclaims you are "taking up too much space if you are not living on the edge."

We get our first glimpse of our sons' primal and untamed nature in the sandbox, where they reign like tiny gods fashioning the world as they go. There we see what an unfettered imagination looks like before society and conformity have begun to snip and tuck, refine, and repress. Working as builders and architects, creators and destroyers, military men and peacemakers, our sons are spontaneous, energetic and original, inventing their world as they go.

Perhaps it was a tiny boy in the sandbox who inspired the ancient Roman writer Themistocles to write: "The wildest colts make the best horses." Rearing his head in the wind, bucking the forces that emphasize what is not possible, a son may one day lead the pack in a rhythmic charge that shakes the world on its axis.

For, well and truly, who would dispute that a son is a gift?

The Gifts a Son Brings

"Why, he's a chip off the old block!"

—A FATHER'S WISH

One evening, while he was building bookcases in his workshop, a carpenter noticed how well his thirteen-year-old son sanded down the rough edges of the wood. "You're a natural with your hands," the man told the boy, with a glint in his eye. "Ever consider what you want to be when you grow up?"

Resting his elbows on the workbench, the young man paused for a minute before answering. "More than anything else, Dad," the son said, "I'd like the chance to be myself, wherever my life and talents take me."

"Of course, my boy," replied the father, somewhat taken aback. "And so you must."

Life is funny. While many parents hope the apple doesn't fall far from the tree, they also expect their sons to "stand on their own two feet" and find their way in the world. Raising a boy who is neither too similar nor too different from themselves seems to be what parents have in mind. "Nobody wants a carbon copy," a mother of a young boy asserted recently. "Every son must develop his own backbone in order to find fulfillment. Even so, I love seeing what my little guy has in common with my husband and me—John's curly hair, my sense of humor. It's proof that he belongs."

If "belonging" has a possessive ring about it—that's the point! Children are often seen through the eyes of their star-gazing parents as prized possessions of the most precious variety. Like prizewinning stallions bred for show, sons are sleek, vibrant, and mercurial creatures who dazzle the crowd as they prance the ring. "Maybe it's narcissistic," one dad commented about his newborn son, "but my wife and I can stand for hours, just watching him sleep. Sometimes we dream of the day our boy will be a man, out in the world, making his own way."

Like the carpenter's son who has a knack for wood, the napping boy may one day surprise his parents by announcing he will blaze a trail where no one in his clan has ever gone. He might, for instance, be the first person in the family to join the ballet or become an artist. Or maybe he will move from the familiar bustle of the city to live in the isolation of a distant wilderness. Stranger things have happened.

Or—as so many parents fantasize—the boy might grow up to be a "chip off the old block." He may decide to "fill dad's shoes," "follow in his footsteps," or "join the firm," as prominent sons throughout history have done.

Going back to ancient times, for instance, Joseph the carpenter was joined in the workshop by a well-known son named Jesus of

"I'd like the chance to be myself..."

Nazareth. Later on in history, the son of the Italian visionary Galileo Galilee became an inventor, as his father before him had. More recently, in the American entertainment industry, father and son actors Kirk and Michael Douglas have shared extraordinary success as stars of the silver screen. And, of course, we have the two George Bushes reaching the political pinnacle of the presidency.

While the famous "like father, like son" duos are many, it is just as thrilling for the Joneses or Johnsons to discover that Billy is athletic and brown eyed—like his father—or left-handed and musical—like his mother. The "bragging rights" that accompanied these new babies home from the hospital are just as strong.

The reason is simple. Deep down inside every human being is a desire to be connected to something larger than ourselves, to be part of a greater whole that helps alleviate and defy the loneliness inherent in the human condition. As one husband and wife so ably put it, "We were a couple until our son was born. Then we became a family." This craving for community may explain why early civilizations banded together in tribes, why family life is the prevalent unit of society, and why a newborn's father boasts, "He's mine. *I made him.* Do you see the likeness?"

Though egotistical pride may seem to belie such remarks, the mystical bond of love is also at work, weaving us together in a living, breathing tapestry of close-knit stitches. For well and truly, a son who makes the world a smaller and more intimate place by "belonging" to those who gave him life is a rare and precious gift.

The Gift of *Immortality*

"He didn't come out of my belly, but my God, I've made his bones."

—JOHN LENNON ON HIS SON

*O*kay contestants, are you ready for a quick quiz? What's the answer to the age-old question, "What's in a name?"

Tick, tick, tick, tick . . .

Give up? Well, when it comes to our sons, the answer is, "Plenty."

According to the *World Book Encyclopedia*, sons are so important in the history of family life that virtually every language on earth has a suffix or prefix meaning "son of." "Irish names beginning with *Mc* or *Mac*, German names ending in *-sohn* or *-son*, and Scandinavian names ending in *-sen* or *-son* all mean 'son of,'" say the editors of the *Encyclopedia*. The same is the case with Russian and Serbian names ending in -*pvitch* and Romanian names ending in -*escy*.

And that's not all. A son's significant role in early history led the ancient Israelites to add "ben" to their given names in order to telegraph that a young man was an important relation of the esteemed patriarch. In the classic movie *Ben Hur*, for instance, which is set in the first-century Middle East, actor Charlton Heston plays a man named Juda ben Hur, who is the son of "Hur."

Surnames also get into the act, helping to establish the primacy of sons. When it comes to the list of names describing the bearer as "the son of John," the *Encyclopedia* includes Johnson and Jackson in

England; Johns and Jones in Wales; Jensen, Jansen, and Hansen in Denmark; Jonsson and Johanson in Sweden; Janowicz in Poland; Icanoc in Russia and Bulgaria; Janosfi in Hungary; and MacEoin in Ireland. Irish names beginning with *O'* signified a grandson.

Whew! That's quite a mouthful. But the point is clear. All around the world, names function as a public broadcast system allowing ferociously proud and possessive families to announce kinship and alert every-body that little junior is a chip off the old block. Like cattle ranchers in the American West who branded their animals with a unique symbol, families throughout time have created surnames to reflect and embrace the identity of their sons.

This habit of taking pride in our sons is long-standing. Going back to the earliest books of the Bible, all of the genealogies from Adam to Noah specifically focus on first sons to reflect their vaunted role in the family. Much more recently, the pride taken in sonship was reflected by the late Beatle, househusband and father John Lennon. "He didn't come out of my belly," the former Beatle boasted, "but my God, I've made his bones because I've attended to every meal, and how he sleeps, and the fact that he swims like a fish because

I took him to the ocean. I'm so proud of all those things. He is my biggest pride."

John Lennon, who died an untimely and tragic death, had named his son Sean, a time-honored variation on his own given name. Though the musician is no longer alive, his son carries on his legacy, offering a little glimpse of the gift of "what's in a name," the precious gift of immortality.

The Gift of
the Apprentice

"'Tis a happy thing to be the father

unto many sons."

—WILLIAM SHAKESPEARE

ring-brinnng! Bring-brinnng! Piercing the morning stillness, the ear-splitting ring of the alarm clock summons a bleary-eyed dad to leave his warm bed and begin the day. Though too tired to acknowledge the wide-eyed boy who has come skipping down the hallway in his cowboy pajamas, dad heads to the bathroom and fills the sink with piping-hot water.

Look! In just seconds, the swirling motion of his soft-bristled brush has created a thick mountain of foamy lather. Spellbound, Junior watches the razor carve tracks in the whipped cream-like cloud Dad has applied to his face. "Darn!" Dad hollers as he nicks

30

himself in a tiny mess-up that sends the small boy scurrying for a bit of tissue paper. Having seen this happen before, our little medic helps stop the thin, red trickle from running down his father's cheek.

"Thanks, partner," calls dad. "Barber Shop special on today. Need a shave?" Mystified by the offer, the boy reaches up to feel the smooth skin of his dad's face, which was coarse and scratchy only hours before when the older man planted a good-night kiss on his fore-head. Dazzled by bathroom light dancing on the edge of the razor, the boy does not reply.

"What do you say, partner, want that shave? No charge for your mustache." Laughing out loud at his

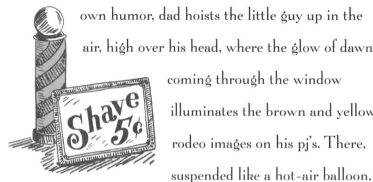

own humor, dad hoists the little guy up in the air, high over his head, where the glow of dawn coming through the window illuminates the brown and yellow rodeo images on his pj's. There, suspended like a hot-air balloon, the boy can see his dad as never before.

"Bye-bye, five o'clock shadow," says dad as he sets his son down. Smelling the aftershave and watching the soap and stubble whirlpool down the drain, the boy knows he will rise early again tomorrow to witness this daily rite. For, in no time at all, he will find himself standing on the threshold of manhood.

The Gift of
the Spittin'
Image

"The spirit and the image…"

—FIFTEENTH-CENTURY PHRASE

When the newborns at County General Hospital were delivered to their parents at feeding time, the maternity nurse handed Mr. Phillips a wriggling blue bundle without checking the name tag. "No doubt about this one," the nurse said with an air of confidence. "This little guy has got to be yours."

"How can you tell?" asked the proud new papa, grinning from ear to ear.

"Spittin' image," the nurse replied.

How many times have you heard that phrase and wondered where it came from? Though "spittin' image" is commonly invoked to mean "exact likeness," few people can explain or even spell the phrase with certainty. And what kind of spit are we talking about, anyway? A barbecue spit that turns round and round over a fire? Or possibly another alternative?

Let's get the spelling issue out of the way first, since the wordsmiths seem to agree that there are several acceptable variations. These include "spit and image,"

"he's the very spirit and image of his father,"

"spitting image," "spitten image" and "spit 'n' image." You can take your pick.

Which still leaves a few important questions to be answered: Where does the phrase "spittin' image" come from and what does it mean?

According to the *QPB Encyclopedia of Word and Phrase Origins,* the expression "spitting image" has been traced back to a fifteenth-century English phrase that reads, "He's as like these as th' has't spit him." Whether that expression meant "he's as like his father as if he had been spit out of his mouth," or was a corruption of "spirit and image" is up for debate, though the evidence favors a blend of both explanations.

Say the editors, a combination "would explain the use of 'and image' in the expression (as it has been used) since the middle of the last century. 'Spitting' image would then be derived from 'he's the very spirit and image of his father,' that is, the child is identical to his parent in both spirit and image. It's possible that both sources combined to give us our phrase for 'exactly alike.'"

So there's an important nuance. To be *exactly like* someone else, we must share their spirit—the invisible component that makes them who they are. Sharing an intangible essence is what the glint in the eye of the "proud papa" is all about, when he holds his newborn son in his arms. Of course it's a thrill to look like our offspring and have our offspring look like us. But, after all, looks are only skin deep. The spirit is far more vast.

So, thank you, Mr. Phillips, for providing a textbook lesson by having a son who offers the gift of the spittin' image.

The Gift of
Pushing Off

*"Growing up requires things one
can push against."*

— TIME

*L*eave me alone!" four-year-old Andrew wailed, as his mother tried to help him on with his rain boots. Though he was late for preschool and had lost the battle with the little yellow wellies that lay on the floor beside him, he was stubborn and defiant. No help, no thanks.

Boys will be boys. And sons will be sons. Especially sons of a certain age. Willfully determined, they reach a point in life where the ferocious desire for self-sufficiency outweighs rhyme, reason, and mom's wish to get to school on time. "I wouldn't mind my son's tenacity if there was any chance he could do the job himself," observed Andrew's mother in frustration.

Nobody ever said that growing up was easy. In fact, an essayist for *Time* magazine once suggested the opposite. "Growing up is a dialectical process that requires things that one can push against in order to become stronger," observed the writer." It takes limited war against worthy opponents. A child matures by testing himself against limits set by loving adults."

Well, now, how many parents knew when they brought their infant sons home from the hospital that they were agreeing to participate in a "limited war"? That in addition to changing diapers, experiencing sleep deprivation and doing mountains of laundry, they were signing on to be a "worthy opponent"? If there are parents who agreed to such a bargain, few would admit it.

And yet, if you ask parents what raising a son is like, war stories will surface. "Sons are a handful, there's no denying it," said a candid mother of three boys. "Full of boundless energy, my little guys are constantly testing me to see how far they can go before I lose my patience and explode."

A child matures by testing himself against limits set by loving adults.

"That's right," another mom in the same play group chimed in. "In a single day, my youngest son can ask the same question a thousand times, get a thousand *no*'s for an answer—and still ask again! If you told me he studied psychological warfare and knew how to bring me to my knees, I would believe it."

Hearing such battle reports makes you wonder why there aren't more orphans in the world! Hand-wringing and hair-pulling are certainly common among well-intentioned parents who are driven to their wit's end by their persistent little boys. Saving moms and dads from dire frustration may be the bountiful supply of love they have on hand to counteract the difficult moments. When child rearing runs the risk of depleting their energy, they dig down deep into their reserves.

"Just when I am about to have a parental meltdown or pack my bags and run away from home," one mom said, "I remember the love I felt the first time I held my son in my arms. Or I look at the notches on the door frame in the kitchen where I keep track of how tall he's grown in just a few years. And I tell myself that this too shall pass."

Isn't it true that time works magic. As every parent of a young boy knows, each passing day brings growth and change to youngsters who act like chicks fighting to crack out of life's eggshell. Picking and pecking ceaselessly, they reach the light when it is least expected. In the meantime, their parents have been taught a lesson in patience and fortitude.

"I try to remind myself that before long Andrew will be able to put his boots on by himself," said his mother. "I only hope that when the day comes, he'll still be interested in doing it!"

Yes, mom, let's hope so. But, in the meantime, always remember an important lesson that child rearing teaches—a son pushing off is a precious gift.

The Gift of
the Hunter
Gatherer

"Sons...stir more than they can quiet."

—SIR FRANCIS BACON

S hopping for clothes with sixteen-year-old John was no fun. When his mother, Mrs. Brown, took him to a department store to buy a new wardrobe for school he would sweep through the place like a fireman on a drill, ferreting out what was "needed" and then beating a hasty retreat to the cash desk.

"Don't you want to browse a little and try a few things on?" Mrs. Brown asked her son. "What if the clothes you picked out don't fit?"

"If the pants are too small," he told his mother efficiently, "I'll bring them back for the next size. If they're too big, I'll wait to grow into them, or wear a belt in the meantime."

"But what about styling?" she asked her son. "You don't know if you like the cut or the way you look in these trousers unless you go to the fitting room."

But, as John's eyes glazed over, Mrs. Brown knew that the conversation—all twenty-five words of it—was over. She paid for her son's purchases and the two proceeded home.

Though it's politically incorrect in some circles to say so, boys are a different breed, especially when it comes to shopping. While mothers and daughters can spend hours in the mall, browsing, preening and trying on clothes they don't need and can't afford, the male approach is different.

"I'd compare it to the hunter-gatherer model," one articulate young man said recently. "When we go shopping we know what we need—the prey. We find it—the hunt. And we make the purchase—the kill. Those are the steps."

Though feminists often contend that male behavior can be molded by a more sensitive upbringing, mothers on the front lines of parenting say otherwise. "When my sons were born," one mother said, "I banned toy guns and swords from the house, allowing only puppets and puzzles. But as soon as the boys could walk, they were picking up sticks and pointing their fingers at each other in a Wild West show. Though it shocked me to admit it, there was really a built-in male operating system."

The rude awakening often dawns soon after mom has filled the baby's room with fluffy stuffed animals that get tossed aside in favor of climbing out of the crib, jumping off the sofa, and crashing toys into each other. Noise, action, and small moving parts rule. Building tall towers and quickly demolishing them illustrates the "warrior gene." Meanwhile the "shopping gene" is nowhere in sight.

"I've given up on trying to change John," says his mother. "And why should I? His practical and goal-oriented approach to life, which I think of as characteristically male, works. He doesn't need to preen in front of the mirror to get the job done."

Yes, indeed. Though John took only a few minutes to select his pants, they fit and he was happy. And, as Mrs. Brown has discovered, a son who doesn't waste time on line for the fitting room is a definite gift!

The Gift of Passage

"You don't raise heroes,

you raise sons."

— WALLY SCHIRRA

*I*n Native American culture, it is called a "vision quest." Among Aboriginal tribes, the term "walkabout" is used. Adolescent Jews marking the transition from boyhood into manhood participate in a ceremony called "bar mitzvah" that combines sacred liturgy and celebration.

Though names may be different, the concept is the same. Rites of initiation into manhood are observed in many societies in carefully prescribed fashion. But what about America? What rite of passage announces that young American boys have assumed responsibility for the life, direction, and well-being of the tribe? And how is their special moment observed?

"I wasn't raised in a particularly religious household," one eighteen-year-old male said recently. "So I guess I would have to say that getting my driver's

license was the closest I came to experiencing an official public passage. But there were many personal moments between my father and me that were

meaningful stepping-stones along the way."

Before learning to drive, many young boys remember dad teaching them to catch a ball, pitch a tent, tie a half-hitch, chop wood, knot a necktie, pack a car, and shave. Dad tossing a baseball in the yard is also a common source of nostalgia. "Sports was definitely a proving ground for me with my dad," a grown son said recently. "Though he never said so, the field, court, or arena was a symbolic combat zone where dad seemed to be preparing his young knight to do battle."

Sometimes, the battle raged as dad attempted to live vicariously through his offspring. The sight of a red-faced man pacing and screaming on the sideline of the field was a signal to young boys that the stakes of the game were high. One day the need to emerge from the shadow of this high-octane cheerleader would prompt them to strike out on their own.

Each son does so in his own time and own way. His rite of passage may take place on a camping trip on which he starts the fire, or in the military, where he shaves his head, becomes part of a fighting machine, and pledges to lay down his life for his comrades. As the drama unfolds, there is the hope that each father will be satisfied with the son who emerges. In the wise words of astronaut Wally Schirra in *Sons*, "You don't raise heroes, you raise sons. And if you treat them like sons, they'll turn out to be heroes, even if it's just in your own eyes."

Those eyes may one day see the tables turn. Later on in life, the child often becomes father to the man. That son may need to put his dad in a nursing home, subsidize his income, or help him shave his wizened face. Assuming full responsibility, as once his father did for him, the son may become the quarterback his father always dreamed to see lead the drive down the field. And he will know that there has been a turnover in the game, that having a son who can carry the ball— literally and figuratively—is a rare and precious gift.

My Son,
My Gift:
What I Love Most
about My Son

*E*very son is special because every son is different. What is unique about yours? The following pages have been provided for you to jot down your special recollections about your son.

Personal Observations about Sons

Resources

Use of the following books is gratefully acknowledged in the research and compilation of this book:

A Book of Love for My Son,
by H. Jackson Brown, Jr. and Hy Brett

A Book of Love for My Daughter,
by H. Jackson Brown, Jr., Paula Y. Flautt, and Kim Shea

A World of Ideas, by Chris Rohmann

Bartlett's Book of Familiar Quotations, 16th edition

Bartlett's Book of Anecdotes, Revised edition

*The Complete Book of Bible Quotations from the
New Testament*, edited by Mark L. Levine and Eugene Rachlis

*The Complete Book of Bible Quotations from the
Old Testament*, edited by Mark L. Levine and Eugene Rachlis

The Fabric of Friendship

Quotationary, by Leonard Roy Frank